T0284083

Incantations

SELECTED BOOKS BY STEVEN NIGHTINGALE

The Paradise Notebooks, co-authored with Dr. Richard Nevle of Stanford. Cornell University Press, 2022.

The Hot Climate of Promises and Grace. Berkeley: Counterpoint Press, 2016.

Granada: A Pomegranate in the Hand of God. Berkeley: Counterpoint Press, 2015.

Edition in the UK: *Granada: The Light of Andalucia.* London: Nicholas Brealey Publishing, 2015.

The Thirteenth Daughter of the Moon. New York: St. Martin's Press, 1996.

The Lost Coast. New York: St. Martin's Press, 1995.

Incantations

DEATHWATCH · WINGS · REVELATION

HAIKU

STEVEN NIGHTINGALE

THE **BLACK SPRING**
PRESS GROUP

First published in 2023
An Eyewear Publishing book, The Black Spring Press Group
Maida Vale, London W9,
United Kingdom

Typeset with graphic design by Edwin Smet
Author photograph Elizabeth Dilly

ISBN 978-1-915406-71-2

The author requested American spelling and usage for this edition.

BLACKSPRINGPRESSGROUP.COM

For Acushla

– la esperanzadora, la bendita, la radiante

CONTENTS

INTRODUCTION — 10

PART I: INFERNO AND THE CURIOUS MIRACLES — 15

PART II: HISTORY AND THE RIVERS OF LIGHT — 101

PART III: RAGE OF NEWS AND LUCENT PEACE — 199

ACKNOWLEDGEMENTS — 262

I am unworthy of the least regard;
yet I am made to rejoice.
—Henry David Thoreau

I don't believe in purity, except for stars and children.
—Enrique Morente

INTRODUCTION

Let us say that a man is in love, and his lover has long hair. It is late in the day, the air is warm and fragrant, and she asks him to braid her hair. He will feel visited by an uncommon and simmering good fortune. He will move behind her and gently take that lovely windfall into his hands and with his fingertips gather slowly her whole mane into three thick strands. Then the braid, finished with a tie or a pin, offers him her neck to kiss. It is the beginning of their night together.

It must be three strands. This slow, amorous commencement of the evening is full of promise and softness. More than that, it holds something deep in the mind that includes them and plays a role in their lives and in all our time on earth: we live by threes.

Think of the most elemental form: lover, beloved, and love itself. Think of the knower, the known, and knowledge itself. Think of the three dimensions of space where we live, and of the first possible way to enclose space within a plane: the triangle of three points.

Einstein's famous equation portrays a cosmic law that describes the proportions by which energy, mass, and light are related. Atoms are composed of protons, neutrons, and electrons. There are three primary colors: red, yellow, and blue. DNA encodes by triplets. Any elastic material cracks into 120-degree angles, dividing that material into three sections. No knot can have fewer than three crossings.

In Christianity, we have the centermost concept of the Trinity, and Dante structured in depth and with fantastic intricacy the whole of *The Divine Comedy* around the number three: it has three parts—the *Inferno*, the *Purgatorio*, and the *Paradiso*, and, not counting the introduction of the whole poem, each part has thirty-three cantos, each canto is composed of the famous *terza rima* of three lines, and those three lines hold thirty-three syllables.

Among the Hindus, we learn of Brahma the Creator, Vishnu the Preserver, and Shiva the Destroyer. In the mystery religion of ancient Egypt we have as principal deities Isis, Osiris, and Horus. In ancient Greece we have the Moirai—the Fates—those three daughters of Gods who made sure that each mortal and each immortal lived out their destiny in accord with cosmic law. The Moirai spin the thread of our lives from a spindle, until the moment when it must be cut.

In poetry, one beautiful use of this principle of three is in Homer, when he plays out a description with three similes. The tercet has been used throughout English poetry—by, say, Shelley in 'Ode to the West Wind', and by the practitioners of the villanelle, which has five tercets followed by a quatrain. In the modern period, both Elizabeth Bishop and Dylan Thomas have given us unforgettable offerings of this form.

For this writer, the most iconic, memorable, and phosphorescent use of the three-line form is in the haiku of Japan. Derived from passionate experimentation beginning in the seventh or eighth century, the form took on its classic powers in the seventeenth century in the work of the legendary Bashō.

I came to haiku later in life. After three decades of writing sonnets, and a year writing verse in the form of questions, as used by Pablo Neruda at the end of his life; after such adventures, I began to write haiku every morning.

It was a scorching, lost, ruined time of life, as if someone had taken a blowtorch and traced each of my veins.

The haiku were a coolness and a liberation. I remember with thankfulness the trustworthy joy each morning as I took pen and notebook in hand. Such a consciously, lovingly made form of verse holds a secret: we can come to dwell within it. And then it slowly heals us.

—SN
The House of Gnomes

Part I

Inferno and the Curious Miracles

A grandfather broken in half
As an example—
Get ready.

Protest will get you
Cut into kibble—
Get ready.

Children paid to juggle
Blasting caps—
Get ready.

Lies like locusts,
Like screaming, like maggots—
Get ready.

Rattlesnakes are rising
Within young men—
Get ready.

A warehouse full
Of severed ears—
Get ready.

They stand in awe
Of beautiful crematoriums—
Get ready.

The colonel loves to fatten
On our children—
Get ready.

Neighbors come, famished,
With filed teeth—
Get ready.

Stomping on throats,
Whipping faces—
Get ready.

High fives after disposing
Of another train-load—
Get ready.

Babies left to bloat
In the sun—
Get ready.

Centerpiece of the library
A case of dynamite—
Get ready.

Made to stand naked,
Rain, winter, midnight—
Get ready.

★★★

I helped you,
Why the hell-broth on high flame—
Hatred.

A morning dissolved
In merciless seething—
Hatred.

Rancor, bitterness,
Brain ablaze, acid-bath—
Hatred.

Soul misshapen,
Pock-marked, suppurating—
Hatred.

Dressing up joyfully
In blood-soaked clothes—
Hatred.

Even candlelight
Diabolical, sulfurous—
Hatred.

Even sunlight ashamed,
Twisted, soiled, failing—
Hatred.

When killing, so important
To lose count—
Hatred.

So many blowtorches,
So few faces—
Hatred.

To use a toothpick
On bits of the neighbor—
Hatred.

A house sinking
Into its own tar-pit—
Hatred.

Let's compare vipers,
Paragons of lovingkindness—
Hatred.

Glass melted down,
Hosed over old men—
Hatred.

Stove left on until
The pots melt—
Hatred.

Fresh food eaten
In front of starving children—
Hatred.

A skull tattoo
On each eyelid—
Hatred.

★★★

A child with
A hand grenade—
    History's edge.

Festival inside
A dead whale—
    History's edge.

Public hangings
Daily at noon sharp—
    History's edge.

A package of maggots
In the mail—
History's edge.

Death in a tuxedo,
Frozen-blood bow tie—
History's edge.

They break our cats
In half—
History's edge.

Cosmetics tested
On young dead men—
History's edge.

Mass graves beneath
The most pious churches—
History's edge.

Mercy mixed in
With sausage meat—
History's edge.

Killers practice, picking off
Teachers and doctors—
History's edge.

Fear for breakfast,
Loathing for lunch—
History's edge.

Every dinner table
A killing field—
History's edge.

Market leaders
In pus and misery—
History's edge.

***

A message—
This world now
A collapsing mineshaft.

A message—
Even the sunlight
Is writhing.

A message—
They'll show how words
Can slit throats.

A message—
Brain tissue gets to love
The blowtorch.

A message—
Candid, bloated, satisfied
Easygoing loathing.

A message—
Every sentence another
Of my severed fingers.

A message—
On paper made
For smoldering.

A message—
Words lined up tidily
Like a firing squad.

A message—
Killing, just so important
To get on with it.

A message—
Explaining how faces
Love a pickaxe.

A message—
Showing how hatred
Loves to gussy up.

A message—
Eyes gouged out, sockets
Filled with crap.

A message—
Good hearts are good
Eaten raw.

A message—
How fun, having
Every stitch ripped out slowly.

★★★

Longing—
A scrub jay's nest
    On my bookshelf.

Longing—
To be entrusted
    With a harvest of honey.

Longing—
Not to be slapped
    For a wisp of hope.

Longing—
One more chance,
　　Barefoot in spring grass.

Longing—
No more sandstorms
　　Ripping skin away.

Longing—
No matter the cold outside,
　　Blazing inside.

Longing—
Just one day not
To be whipped.

★★★

The killing stopped,
Owls on the windowsill—
If only.

No more sequined
Festivals of death and candy—
If only.

No girl anywhere in fear
Of a man, ever—
If only.

Flags abandoned in favor
Of girls and souls—
If only.

Every gun melted down
To make bird feeders—
If only.

Young men instructed
By young women—
If only.

All gold at the ready
To buy books and ice cream—
If only.

Gentleness that can be
Tasted in the air—
If only.

A woman in love
Means what she says—
If only.

Emily Dickinson knocks
At the door—
If only.

A family of foxes asleep
On the sofa—
If only.

Old man's mind
A tumult of rainbows—
If only.

Old woman's mind
All trust, oceans, and wonder—
If only.

History never again
A rotting tapestry of hatred—
If only.

School every day
All joy and jailbreak—
If only.

Weapons all cashed in
For rivers and libraries—
If only.

★★★

Cannibals in coat and tie
Holding neutron bombs—
No more.

Girls pinned down,
Cut between the legs—
No more.

Young men aglow with
Bayonets, medals, flamethrowers—
No more.

Classrooms putrid
With lies and contempt—
No more.

Icepick used
For prefrontal lobotomy—
No more.

Mass grave, the murdered
Still screaming—
No more.

Book ripped from
The hands of a little girl—
No more.

Prisons, coal plants,
Refugee camps—
No more.

Television like
Dressed-up excrement—
No more.

Heads of state
Intestinal, repugnant, proud—
No more.

Luxury goods glazed
With loathing—
No more.

Entertainment fabricated
Like heroin, like crack—
No more.

The bonfire prepared
For books and children—
No more.

Heaven turns its face
From us in shame—
No more.

★★★

Made of grass,
Birdsong, starlight—
A way forward.

Illuminated rough wild
Country inside a book—
A way forward.

Having nothing without,
To have something within—
A way forward.

Following the owls
Deep into a canyon—
A way forward.

Climbing a ladder
Into the stratosphere—
A way forward.

A deep exhaustion
That is kindling—
A way forward.

All light exploding
In a piece of quartz—
A way forward.

The sunlight
Everywhere, signaling—
A way forward.

The source of light
Has itself a source—
A way forward.

Riffs, answers, ideas,
Even in the ashes—
A way forward.

Distant wisp of light
Every incendiary perfection—
A way forward.

Learning the dance steps
Into my own vanishing—
   A way forward.

Family of lions waiting
In the front yard—
   A way forward.

The last of twilight has
A taste of nutmeg—
   A way forward.

Gone off with trade winds,
With the jetstream—
A way forward.

Next world unfolding
In frost on the window—
A way forward.

★★★

Can it be the time
To build on the ruins of this heart—
Jailbreak.

So what if every bone has been
Slowly twisted and broken—
Jailbreak.

No longer available
For the morning noose—
Jailbreak.

They'll miss the chance
To take another of my fingers—
Jailbreak.

They'll scrub down my cell,
Contaminated territory—
    Jailbreak.

The memory of me
They'll mix with vomit—
    Jailbreak.

Exultant to walk upon
This hard infinite alkali plain—
    Jailbreak.

Makes me laugh when they
Trumpet about finding me—
        Jailbreak.

I'll be in the eighth day
Of the week—
        Jailbreak.

I'll be in the fortieth day
Of the month—
        Jailbreak.

I'll be in the millennium after
The next twenty—
    Jailbreak.

I'll be reveling on the earth
Hidden inside this earth—
    Jailbreak.

I'll be swinging
On a trapeze between stars—
    Jailbreak.

With a bar that held me
I'll vault onto a mountaintop—
    Jailbreak.

In the distance I'll turn
Into fireflies—
    Jailbreak.

There is a new constellation,
The Open Door—
    Jailbreak.

★★★

Pathways inside silence,
Justice delicious everywhere—
Escape route.

Even one snowflake,
One phosphorescent book—
Escape route.

Even in flammable disaster,
Even through polluted rage—
Escape route.

Going slow, leaving behind
Breakneck lethal news—
    Escape route.

In a house finch,
Firestorm of answers—
    Escape route.

A hummingbird who holds
Every summer everywhere—
    Escape route.

In one dry brown leaf,
Cyclone of secrets—
Escape route.

Short word broken apart
To show worlds infinite—
Escape route.

Jagged pandemonium gives in
To rapture of necessary laughter—
Escape route.

Quiet morning, clear streaming
Titanic ways forward—
    Escape route.

Able to make a refuge
Anywhere, at any time—
    Escape route.

All heaven at home
In a dust mote—
    Escape route.

All sky and ocean packed
Into one piece of lapis—
    Escape route.

Firelight healing with
Its golden lotions—
    Escape route.

Foxes at play showing
Every flourishing kingdom—
    Escape route.

From within this devotion
Dream-wings may be made—
Escape route.

★★★

Glance across the room,
Just one—
Tipping point.

A side canyon, dusty,
Quiet, colossal—
Tipping point.

Morning, outside, writing
A sonnet, cougar in the grass—
Tipping point.

Aspen grove, waking with
A lover, coyote next to us—
Tipping point.

Green eddy, water clear,
Reflecting twenty centuries—
Tipping point.

Candlelight, one dinner,
Upwelling of trust—
　　Tipping point.

One teacher, her books,
Her way of loving—
　　Tipping point.

Boy in the forest, resin
Showing all gold everywhere—
　　Tipping point.

High Sierra lake,
Seven waterfalls, moonlight—
Tipping point.

Cut to pieces, assembled
Myself in solitude—
Tipping point.

Random day, chance word
About a cabin on a river—
Tipping point.

The book like holding
An ocean in my hand—
Tipping point.

Learning to be still,
Cyclones of soul turning—
Tipping point.

One friend, one day
Came to help once—
Tipping point.

A cream made of salt
And musk and heaven—
Tipping point.

★★★

Breakthrough—
The meadow with wildflowers
On the moon.

Breakthrough—
The fawn asleep
In my reading chair.

Breakthrough—
Galaxies consulting
　　With a white poppy.

Breakthrough—
Bristlecone pine whose
　　Branches conduct history.

Breakthrough—
The new moon hiding
　　In our library.

Breakthrough—
The way morning light
Loves a broken mind.

Breakthrough—
Constellations in the palm
Of our hands.

Breakthrough—
In every blade of grass
Boisterous theology.

Breakthrough—
Paw-prints of a bobcat
Across my dreams.

Breakthrough—
The kite on the ground
Flies me.

Breakthrough—
In a hot air balloon, stopping
At every planet.

Breakthrough—
Stampede of wild horses
Over our notebooks.

Breakthrough—
The blue jay flying around
In my brain.

Breakthrough—
Visiting my own body
Only when called.

Breakthrough—
Hummingbirds nesting
   In violins and saxophones.

Breakthrough—
Death came around, what
   A little twerp.

***

One scrub jay,
One dust mote—
   The antidote.

Cooking, even once,
For a beloved—
The antidote.

One night, seven dreams
Of wings and light—
The antidote.

One winged seed
Of one maple—
The antidote.

A peach pit, with
Its little canyonlands—
The antidote.

Quiet day, cataracts
Roaring in the house—
The antidote.

A walk around the block,
Deliverance and tempests—
The antidote.

The cat comes
With cash from heaven—
The antidote.

The morning when reality
Takes off its clothes—
The antidote.

Birdsong, tuning fork
For the universe—
The antidote.

Wind in the big oak
Brushing away all hatred—
The antidote.

In a meadow, moonlight
Plays with a filly—
The antidote.

Onshore breeze, soft
Rampage of sensuality—
The antidote.

Pine cone, communicating
With pinwheel galaxies—
The antidote.

One sentence in a book,
Fireworks all day in the mind—
The antidote.

Death comes, you
Wait with handfuls of cinnamon—
The antidote.

★★★

This morning—
I meet a weaver, one galaxy
Threaded into another.

This morning—
Blessings like a tremor
And invitation of earth.

This morning—
Music of the spheres brought
By soft rainfall.

This morning—
The owls offer a cosmos
From faraway bell towers.

This morning—
Seeing who delivers gold
To all the honeycombs.

This morning—
A language to learn, spoken
By grass, clouds, coyotes.

This morning—
In mossy branching of one oak,
Prophecy and history.

This morning—
Shy hopeful phrases hiding
In the sage petals.

This morning—
Drawing new constellations
In the dirt.

This morning—
Doing standup comedy, to an audience
Of crows.

This morning—
Ocean currents course
Through hands and heart.

This morning—
Into another house, another
Life, another world.

This morning—
Shafts of light in a forest
The keys of a piano.

This morning—
Antics of swallows, circus
That is learning.

***

This afternoon—
The taproot touches
Reality once again.

This afternoon—
All dust is
Diamond dust.

This afternoon—
A baby asleep, with
A safeguard of galaxies.

This afternoon—
One friend, one visit,
Exultant safety.

This afternoon—
One grass blade,
Arc of all blessing.

This afternoon—
Perfect internal tempest,
Plainsong of education.

This afternoon—
Destiny turns up,
Wants to talk.

This afternoon—
The whole morning present
In every second.

This afternoon—
The cats bring home
A saint.

This afternoon—
An eagle flies in
From the zenith of dreams.

This afternoon—
A manual of instructions
From the stars.

This afternoon—
Food that makes
Fatigue into beauty.

This afternoon—
Wine that tastes
Like trust and safety.

This afternoon—
Poetry that has
Even the moon listening.

★★★

The next world breezes
Through the door—
This refuge.

Rivers of fire offhandedly
Turned aside—
This refuge.

The whole house full
Of water ouzels—
This refuge.

Eagles nest
On the bookshelf—
This refuge.

Every word sewn with
Infinite golden threads—
This refuge.

Madness breaks the mind
With beauties—
This refuge.

Socrates here, blowing
Bubbles, tying balloons—
This refuge.

On the page, archipelago
Of stars—
This refuge.

Can send the soul out
To look around—
This refuge.

My whole life
Now helpful kindling—
This refuge.

Body's tryout of death
Ignites the mind—
This refuge.

Opening a book onto
Future centuries—
This refuge.

Opening a book, beginning
Another universe—
This refuge.

Heart knows where
The soul is going—
This refuge.

Suffering: both terror
And clarity—
This refuge.

Heart valves curve like
Horizon at twilight—
This refuge.

In deep space, and
Within a fingertip—
This refuge.

★★★

Depth charges
At the base of the brain—
Sweetness.

Bookshelf nearby,
Coffee, touch, memory, longing—
Sweetness.

On a walk, not even
One napalm strike—
Sweetness.

Thinking maybe tomorrow
I'll still be alive—
Sweetness.

Opening the door,
Her incandescence again—
Sweetness.

Opening the door,
Thunderbolt of her beauty—
Sweetness.

Walking hand in hand,
Wind in the trees—
Sweetness.

Stories like a blueprint
Of worlds within this one—
Sweetness.

Talk, wings, love, books,
Cooking, cherished work—
Sweetness.

Surety of love like
Daily sheet lightning—
Sweetness.

Understanding comes
Like a spring river—
Sweetness.

Learning how heaven
Has never been shy—
Sweetness.

Mare and foal
In the front yard—
Sweetness.

My failures taken out
With the garbage—
Sweetness.

Banking internal fire
So heat and light can be called—
Sweetness.

Wrapped up together afterwards,
Love's impossible geometry—
Sweetness.

Part II
History and the Rivers of Light

Tattoos, guns, swagger,
Suit and tie—
Every day.

Awake and eager
For someone to pulverize—
Every day.

No festive musical revelry
Like our humiliation—
Every day.

Looking for a school
To abominate, to incinerate—
Every day.

They'll enslave us,
Call us pretty lilting names—
Every day.

Questions about justice
Answered with a jackhammer—
Every day.

A dog torn to pieces
Before dinner—
Every day.

Teachers chosen for
The shooting gallery—
Every day.

Training the vultures
To eat us alive—
Every day.

Testing their knives
On our tongues and eyes—
Every day.

The scholars lecture
On the minutiae of loathing—
Every day.

With needles writing slowly
Their lies into our skin—
Every day.

Watching the coyotes
Toy with an infant—
Every day.

Seething of maggots
Their favorite cinema—
Every day.

Their garden a breeding ground
Of cankers and tumors—
Every day.

Fury and rancid contempt
For flowers, stars, children—
Every day.

★★★

Days a sinkhole,
History a sinkhole—
Nausea.

Damburst of lies,
Every house a slaughterhouse—
Nausea.

Children at the grocery store
On the meathooks—
Nausea.

Crimson poison simmering
On clean new stovetops—
Nausea.

They say extermination
Is the sporting life—
Nausea.

Snipers with assignments,
One hundred and one a day—
Nausea.

Senator covering the monster
With sequins and spangles—
Nausea.

Music made to run
In sewer pipes only—
Nausea.

The screaming of men
Marinated in hatred—
Nausea.

Men chosen for
Excremental qualities—
Nausea.

They feel much better
When they eat our fresh brains—
Nausea.

Making catastrophe
Into a food group—
Nausea.

They want us to beg
For decapitation—
Nausea.

They say bloodlust
Is the last and only glamour—
Nausea.

They say mutilation
Is noble bloodsport—
    Nausea.

They say terror can be
Taken beautifully to the bank—
    Nausea.

    ★★★

Hard cash a narcotic, love
The art of humiliation—
    Deathwatch.

A fury metallic, cold,
Lethal, wealthy, sentimental—
    Deathwatch.

Their fun is snapping wings
From small birds—
    Deathwatch.

Filling a brokerage account by
Calculations of hatred—
    Deathwatch.

Lining up friends
For target practice—
    Deathwatch.

Tattooed muscles swollen from
Work of extermination—
    Deathwatch.

Lash of the whip always
Across open eyes—
    Deathwatch.

Front lawns so convenient
For killing fields—
Deathwatch.

Vampire bats ashamed
Of every one of us—
Deathwatch.

Turning gears so ingenious
In the factory of pure terror—
Deathwatch.

Like spices in a rack,
Their beloved weapons lined up—
Deathwatch.

There is the anvil where
Dreams are pounded to pulp—
Deathwatch.

New choral music
Made for screaming only—
Deathwatch.

Their hope is somehow to make
Heaven bleed to death—
Deathwatch.

★★★

Icepick in my
Open wound—
There they go.

Waking me up, so they
Can burn me again—
There they go.

Killing me,
Their aperitif—
There they go.

Sunlight just
A big fraud—
There they go.

I'll love it, being
Pulverized—
There they go.

Planting mushrooms
In my eye sockets—
There they go.

Days just so tedious
Without torture—
There they go.

Reptiles
In coats and ties—
There they go.

A factory to make
Agony into food—
There they go.

Making trust into
Gutter trash—
There they go.

Watching what insects
Will do to me—
There they go.

The fiend with
Beautiful cufflinks—
There they go.

For every child,
Fawning and loathing—
There they go.

What an adornment, their
Pestilential joy—
There they go.

★★★

Manacled to silence,
Ransacked by shadows—
Heartsick.

Heaven moving away,
Ever faster, every day—
Heartsick.

Friends with ax-heads,
Whips, pliers, contempt—
Heartsick.

Waking up, the mind
Gaping and pillaged—
Heartsick.

Afternoon, what is this
Rat's nest in my guts—
Heartsick.

They sauté my brains
In butter and sage—
Heartsick.

My body parts sold as
Gift-wrapped burnt offerings—
Heartsick.

They loved my physique,
One limb at a time—
Heartsick.

They think I'm handsome,
Trussed in chains and filthy—
Heartsick.

A new language, it means
Blessing is bloodlust—
Heartsick.

The screw in my face
Turned once a week, on Sunday—
Heartsick.

Showing video
Of my slow dismemberment—
Heartsick.

Do they think I do not know
The florid spectrum of pain—
Heartsick.

They clap every hour
When I am carved—
Heartsick.

★★★

Every window in
Every house broken—
Glamorous.

All of your friends
Watch their guts pulled out—
Glamorous.

Practicing their backhand
Across faces—
Glamorous.

Making a world safe
For stacked corpses—
Glamorous.

Suit buttons made from
Fingernails of children—
Glamorous.

Welding shut the gates
Of heaven—
Glamorous.

Let's give a fair chance
To hell on earth—
Glamorous.

Staff up to match
The plans for murder—
Glamorous.

Justice is being able
To say who dies—
Glamorous.

In art school, everyone working
With fresh rib cages—
Glamorous.

Stabbing now by textbook
Or sophisticated freestyle—
Glamorous.

Teaching everyone how fear
Is the best food—
Glamorous.

Nothing becomes a man
Like meticulous loathing—
Glamorous.

Saving all the napalm
For libraries—
Glamorous.

★★★

They'll eat my dog,
Then me—
Happy guys.

Filling the ledger,
Pens dipped in strychnine—
Happy guys.

A sick baby,
Stomped to death—
Happy guys.

Bidding for
The best whores—
Happy guys.

Life a mess,
But money, exquisite—
Happy guys.

They have servants
Cook history to their taste—
Happy guys.

They watch prisoners
Whip each other to death—
Happy guys.

Our suffering just one more
After-dinner mint—
Happy guys.

★★★

A knock at the door,
Key in an envelope—
It's time.

One door slammed,
Eight doors open wide—
It's time.

Invited into the den
Of burrowing owls—
It's time.

Invited to eat berries
With the black bear—
It's time.

Opening the newspaper,
It turns into wings—
It's time.

In a phrase, seven seas,
The source of all winds—
It's time.

Scrub jay's call
Cracks open the mind—
It's time.

Cheetah family asleep
Around the writing desk—
It's time.

New constellations
In the sky every night—
It's time.

Desire lost, found
Only in love aloft—
It's time.

Afternoon dust-motes'
Slow concerto and ballet—
It's time.

Finally, trust, our blessed
Everyday peaceable firestorm—
It's time.

Leaves blowing in the street
Towards origin and destiny—
It's time.

In wretched calamity,
The affable typhoon we need—
It's time.

The soul a stormfront
Of premonition and blessing—
It's time.

Around a fingertip,
Ring-dance of stars—
It's time.

★★★

Tornado—
Come to turn mind
Inside out.

Tornado—
Within him, at
The thought of her.

Tornado—
In the tissue
Of morning verses.

Tornado—
Turning the body
Into the sky.

Tornado—
Inside the spine, now
We stand straight.

Tornado—
Tunnel to the zenith
Waiting for you.

Tornado—
Windswept life, ready
For a windswept death.

Tornado—
Undersong to your
Tranquil phrase.

★★★

Lightning—
Out for a walk,
      Like everyone else.

Lightning—
Makes thunder, then
      Mischievously hides.

Lightning—
Just has to practice
      That dance step.

Lightning—
Trying to throw
A net for heaven.

Lightning—
And the foals everywhere
Get onto their feet.

Lightning—
Showing what a line
Of thought can do.

Lightning—
Playing hide and seek
With the world.

Lightning—
Neurons firing
In paradise.

★★★

The first shining,
Our only road—
Ocean.

Azure exaltations,
Old cosmos—
Ocean.

Trustworthy rhythm,
Erotic intimation—
Ocean.

Sitting close with you,
Making salt and light—
Ocean.

Waves curling
Into the next world—
Ocean.

Playing a tambourine
In every galaxy—
Ocean.

Beauty broken,
Then unbroken—
Ocean.

At centermost of love,
Motion of salt, light, lapis—
Ocean.

Falling together,
Rolling back home together—
Ocean.

Just the way
You glisten—
Ocean.

Even asleep, horizons
Of moving light in you—
    Ocean.

Shore-bound, sky-bound,
Light-bound—
    Ocean.

Knowing that salt,
Your salt—
    Ocean.

Both our longing
And our consummation—
Ocean.

Everywhere we travel
And our home-ground—
Ocean.

★★★

Sleep—
One night, dreams.
Another, daggers.

Sleep—
Waits like a lover,
Then like an assassin.

Sleep—
Dreams come, merciful
Wings, the whirling.

Sleep—
Dreams only
Can be trusted.

Sleep—
The last blessing
Left.

Sleep—
Awakening
In a distant galaxy.

Sleep—
Through a portal
Vanishing at last.

Sleep—
Dreams enveloping,
Volcanic, convulsive.

Sleep—
Where it's safe
To bleed.

Sleep—
Riding around the sky
On winged lions.

Sleep—
Seminar, taught by
A billion stars.

Sleep—
Water running
Uphill.

Sleep—
Off to cities constructed
By a lover.

Sleep—
Finally at home
In a supernova.

Sleep—
Decades strung
Like a cello.

Sleep—
Clear dreaming cut-loose
Floodtide of beauties.

★★★

A phrase in a book
That sought your hand—
Winged seeds.

Sunlight on a river
Roaring through dreams—
Winged seeds.

Waking in darkness
And our salty surety—
Winged seeds.

Waves of original ocean
Curl within our notebook—
Winged seeds.

Bread baking,
Kissing in the kitchen—
Winged seeds.

One glance, one word,
One touch, just in time—
Winged seeds.

Mischievous journeywork
Through delicious sheets—
Winged seeds.

Holding each other
Aloft together—
Winged seeds.

Even in history
Like hot tar—
Winged seeds.

Even in the chambers
Of torture we have catalogued—
Winged seeds.

Even if drinking cups
Hold steaming poison—
Winged seeds.

Even diving into a pool
Of melted sulfur—
Winged seeds.

Even when death
Galumphed across the room—
Winged seeds.

Hot day, juice of lime
In a glass of rum—
Winged seeds.

In the morning air
Open secret answering passageways—
Winged seeds.

Every deep root knows
The directives of heaven—
Winged seeds.

★★★

Even in pandemonium
And tar-pit of contempt—
Safety.

Candlelight, firelight, daylight,
Lovemaking light—
Safety.

Living within
Ancient radiance of stories—
Safety.

We can tell the mirror
Whether or not to reflect—
Safety.

Cinnamon and nutmeg
Our boon companions—
Safety.

Pawprints of cats
Across our dreams—
Safety.

We call winter storms,
Then a tropical atoll—
Safety.

Owl, fox, bobcat
Come to muse with us—
Safety.

Together watching
The watchful light—
Safety.

Ready dreaming headwaters
Take form in us—
Safety.

Our lives together a river
Who knows about the ocean—
Safety.

Words, touch, truth,
Dreams, work, paradise—
Safety.

Whirling so that we
Land within one another—
Safety.

Allspice, trust, wings, heat,
Our simmering of reality—
Safety.

★★★

Finally, the company,
The time, the place—
We're ready.

Unmistakable surging
Inside of starlight—
We're ready.

Transcendental alarm clock
Gone off in the soul—
We're ready.

Flowers delivered
From another planet—
We're ready.

Taking our time, choosing
Among flying carpets—
We're ready.

The clocks stopped, all time
Rang open—
We're ready.

Scar-bound mind finally
Come to freedom once again—
We're ready.

Letting soul saunter away
From the body—
We're ready.

Hope alive, without
Arsenic of expectation—
We're ready.

Our words riding a wave
Like dolphins—
We're ready.

Reading stories aloud,
Wildflowers of the mind—
We're ready.

Reading stories aloud,
Meteor showers in the room—
We're ready.

Reading stories aloud,
Unfolding love's gracenotes—
We're ready.

Fire in the hearth, rising
Together in hot light—
We're ready.

We hand over our treasures,
Each other's beloved custodian—
We're ready.

All our days now
Open fateful homeland—
We're ready.

★★★

From within the world
That's within the mind—
Because of you.

Clouds, moonlight,
Poetry, mayflies—
Because of you.

Insects know about
Visiting galaxies—
　　Because of you.

Alkali plain embraced
By the rain forest—
　　Because of you.

River currents running
Through a book—
　　Because of you.

Rosemary bush growing
In a book—
Because of you.

Grass in wind writing
A book of spells—
Because of you.

Conscious beautiful
Sleepless dreaming—
Because of you.

At home, on the way
To deep space—
    Because of you.

The question
Within all questions—
    Because of you.

The answer
To all our answers—
    Because of you.

Oceans lost
In a raindrop—
Because of you

Stormfront inside
The honey jar—
Because of you.

Justice walks
Free in the street—
Because of you.

Redwood seeds full
Of incandescent prayer—
Because of you.

One shooting star
Wipes away all hatred—
Because of you.

★★★

Storytelling of seasons,
Epic in a spice pod—
Tell me.

Snowflakes ablaze
In a gust of golden light—
Tell me.

Would you carry on, close
To me, aloft with me—
Tell me.

How you kindle within you
Such slow-fired hungry grace—
Tell me.

Do you see paradise present,
Open, sassy, known, ardent—
Tell me.

How is it my hands
Are shaped for your face only—
Tell me.

Will you travel with me
To the cosmos in a dust-mote—
Tell me.

In the kitchen with me
Will you cook up a world—
    Tell me.

Will you touch wings today,
Tonight, tomorrow, just now—
    Tell me.

Will you move with me in canyons
Enfolding us in sheets of stone—
    Tell me.

Would you go with me far
Into the exultation of invisibility—
Tell me.

Would you vanish with me
Into this beautiful privacy—
Tell me.

Is life learning there is no
Creation save shared creation—
Tell me.

Do you see how
Withholding kills revelation—
Tell me.

Would you dream with me
Until our dreams walk free—
Tell me.

How is it two souls can
Come home to raw worldly joy—
Tell me.

★★★

Desert lake, delivery
And directive of wings—
This vanishing.

Keys in our hands,
Doors in the sky—
This vanishing.

All the crows flying
Away with darkness—
This vanishing.

Ocean currents surging
In dreams at morning—
This vanishing.

To give everything, then
To give the nothing left—
This vanishing.

Darkness so concentrated
It turns into light—
This vanishing.

Even sideways freezing rain
Inconceivably beautiful—
This vanishing.

Nothing left for suffering
To work on—
This vanishing.

So sorry, all you
Demons and godforsaken furies—
This vanishing.

So sorry, all you
Warlocks and fat gorgons—
This vanishing.

The earth itself
A magic talisman—
This vanishing.

The horizon itself
A magic ring—
This vanishing.

Sunlight itself
A language meant for us—
This vanishing.

A time bomb
Exploding into life—
This vanishing.

Eternity in old clothes,
Ambling down the street—
This vanishing.

When a body naked
Is a naked soul—
        This vanishing.

★★★

Better to have death
As sidekick and raconteur—
        Resurgence.

The Furies sucking
Their teeth in disappointment—
        Resurgence.

What if deep defiance
Is peaceable and musical—
Resurgence.

What if faintest starlight
Is uncontrollably lustrous in the mind—
Resurgence.

It's the talons of gravity,
Or trusting life to wings—
Resurgence.

The very last of the last
Of last chances—
Resurgence.

Here is my life, here,
Love, is all of it—
Resurgence.

I would be worth
One gleam on a goldfinch's wing—
Resurgence.

Wakefulness every day
Like a solar flare—
Resurgence.

Wind on fire, moving beauty
Making brain into mind—
Resurgence.

Knowing the first name
Of every star—
Resurgence.

Knowing the first name
Of every grass blade—
Resurgence.

Centuries of clear spring sky
Packed into a piece of lapis—
Resurgence.

A late catnap, wrapped
In the buckskin sunset—
Resurgence.

The dictionary opens
To the hundredth name of heaven—
Resurgence.

The library always ready
To carouse with us—
Resurgence.

Dead brown leaf pile
Crackling with answers—
Resurgence.

Silence, vanishing, joy
Like allspice on fire—
Resurgence.

Cold winter branches bare
And coursing with dreams—
Resurgence.

Rotating the kaleidoscope,
Heaven keeps turning up—
Resurgence.

Heaven and earth,
Warp and weft—
Resurgence.

***

At the door, a visitor
From beyond the stars—
Unity.

River system
In muscle fiber—
Unity.

A blue whale
Replaces every cathedral—
Unity.

Rain forest
From the floorboards—
Unity.

Glacier
In a snowflake—
Unity.

Tempest
In a fingertip—
Unity.

Ten years compressed
Into one second—
Unity.

Late twilight held
In tawny rum—
Unity.

Bronze moon
In the living room—
Unity.

Meadowlarks nesting
On the moon—
Unity.

Cats running along
The rings of Saturn—
Unity.

Holy book tucked
Inside a mustard seed—
Unity.

Sand dunes moving
In a shot glass—
Unity.

Morning light
Surprising midnight—
Unity.

The fox watching
You work—
Unity.

The crossbow loaded
With solar flares—
Unity.

Part III
Rage of News
and Lucent Peace

Don't think. We'll
Have to impale you—
We're sorry.

Forget morning. Who
Do you think you are?
We're sorry.

Your dreams, now
Food for pigs—
We're sorry.

Joy is what
Makes you stupid—
We're sorry.

Love is what marks you
For slaughter—
We're sorry.

History is cookware.
Your hopes, frying—
We're sorry.

Your little struggle,
So epileptic, so pathetic—
We're sorry.

Our love will come
To snuff you out—
We're sorry.

You can tell a good book,
Pages stuck together with blood—
We're sorry.

Burnt at the stake,
Books for fuel—
We're sorry.

A little bit of blowtorch
Every day—
We're sorry.

Stuffing your eyes
With cheap thrills and trinkets—
We're sorry.

News to rub you
To death with sandpaper—
We're sorry.

Death, a package deal,
You and your children—
We're sorry.

★★★

The news from here—
Lava is filling
The house.

The news from here—
Horned and steaming
Visitors every day.

The news from here—
It's burning today.
It will burn tomorrow.

The news from here—
They tutor children until
The screaming does not stop.

The news from here—
It's normal, the implacable
Daily thrill of sadism.

The news from here—
They make sure we
Suffer in public.

The news from here—
Grenade forced in my mouth,
Now what?

The news from here—
So many recipes
For my hands.

The news from here—
Mint of hatred
Pounding out money.

The news from here—
They detest our dying
Just once.

The news from here—
I have to tie
My own noose.

The news from here—
Heartsick, mind-sick,
World-sick.

The news from here—
Death, good, at last someone
To trust.

The news from here—
They have everything.
They will have it always.

★★★

They did not walk,
They ran to their death—
Fact.

Gun muzzle in the mouth
Every morning—
Fact.

Voted for the one
Who hated them most—
Fact.

Loved a family as they
Watched them burn—
Fact.

Made an appointment
To be decapitated—
Fact.

Gave blood until
It was gone—
Fact.

Tested the jackhammer
On teachers—
Fact.

County fair, carvings
From fresh brains—
Fact.

Napalm used at random,
On nursing homes—
Fact.

No one goes anywhere
Without a best-loved gun—
Fact.

Every university
Sown with land mines—
Fact.

Death and hatred have
A good laugh together—
Fact.

An hour of killing,
Then back to budgets—
Fact.

Everybody's number shows
How much they'll suffer—
Fact.

Winter, freezing, the old
Paraded around naked—
Fact.

Television like being
Fed our own intestines—
Fact.

★★★

Sorrow—
Molten lead
At the brain stem.

Sorrow—
Pile driver timed
    To my pulse.

Sorrow—
Brute guttural motion
    Of the blood.

Sorrow—
Razor wire cinched
    Tighter every day.

Sorrow—
Every love-gift
Returned, detested.

Sorrow—
Packages in the mail,
Each one empty.

Sorrow—
Letter in the mail,
Pages blank.

Sorrow—
One morning after another
    Into the trash compactor.

Sorrow—
Snuffing out every one
    Of love's candles.

Sorrow—
The clock won't
    Stop chiming.

Sorrow—
Air raid siren
        Won't stop screaming.

Sorrow—
Snow falls until
        The city disappears.

Sorrow—
Earth splits, chasm
        Through the house.

Sorrow—
Every waterfall
Frozen in place.

Sorrow—
Stove lit,
The cook dead.

★★★

The furies give up,
Melt down their weapons—
Blazing.

Even by candlelight,
By first bare morning light—
Blazing.

A place, a story,
A hope, touch, silence—
Blazing.

A step inside is
A step outside—
Blazing.

A book in hand,
A story read aloud—
Blazing.

Fate comes around
With muscles of honey—
Blazing.

Opening our wings
Together and together—
Blazing.

We see doors
Ajar in distant jubilant cities—
Blazing.

Heaven is here,
Amorous, lovely, amused—
Blazing.

An old proverb offers
A hand, a light, an idea—
Blazing.

Conjuring the heat
We need to learn—
Blazing.

Even in languor after love,
Even in dreams—
Blazing.

We write on paper given
To the hearth of every second—
Blazing.

The sun in the sky,
In a phrase, in our dreams—
Blazing.

When our answers touch
Our questions—
Blazing.

★★★

Silence, even silence,
Alone with her—
Revelation.

Moonlight liquid along
Infinite sand dunes—
Revelation.

Any seed in the hand
Of any child—
Revelation.

Any wave, any beach,
Any day—
Revelation.

My flesh transparent
To the animals—
    Revelation.

    Dragonflies
In the late-river light—
    Revelation.

    Each raindrop
Journeywork of millennia—
    Revelation.

Time in our hands
Like clay—
        Revelation.

Somersaulting into
The next world—
        Revelation.

Every word
Its own supernova—
        Revelation.

Stories made for
Mind's planetary turning—
Revelation.

Leaving myself in the gutter,
Walking away in joy—
Revelation.

Pulling self off myself
Like a soiled costume—
Revelation.

Loving a match,
My life now kindling—
Revelation.

The way fingertips find
A way to deep space—
Revelation.

★★★

Make bed sheets from
Silken fragrant trade winds—
Let's.

Hitchhike together on the way
To every heaven that will have us—
Let's.

Make common cause
With crows and supernovas—
Let's.

Tap-dance and scat-sing along
The asteroid belt—
Let's.

Vanish into daily
Planetary shenanigans—
Let's.

Work in the factory
Where snowflakes are made—
Let's.

Open the door wide
When destiny knocks—
Let's.

Set the furies to work
Ice fishing—
Let's.

Practice our dashing
With a foal in open country—
Let's.

Gambol with coyotes
Through the national library—
Let's.

Sleep with owls
At the top of a cottonwood—
Let's.

Write choral music
Using only whispers—
Let's.

Lift a candelabra to light
A new constellation—
Let's.

Sail a clipper ship
Through history and the future—
Let's.

Vanish together into
Our handmade homeland—
Let's.

★★★

Wings were there within
The whole time—
Flying.

Dreams and daylight
Laced together in this love—
Flying.

All of earth asks us
Just to learn, only that—
Flying.

Looking for her
To touch wings—
Flying.

So slow it is beyond
The velocity of light—
Flying.

Everyplace we go, knowing
Where to find the honeycomb—
Flying.

Making candlelight
Into interior light—
Flying.

It's time to go, or
It's time to die—
Flying.

★★★

World healed again,
Every minute, every day—
Just here.

Crack between worlds,
Heaven pouring in—
Just here.

One phrase holds
A hundred galaxies—
Just here.

Hope touches off
A conflagration of blessings—
Just here.

A little goldfinch visits,
Fresh from paradise—
Just here.

A book in mind simmered,
Tastes like all beauty—
Just here.

Hand in hand is
World in world—
Just here.

Conversation that curves
Sinuous as a river—
Just here.

A hundred dragonflies
Weaving together the century—
Just here.

Clothes off slowly,
Spring river currents—
Just here.

★★★

Sunlight in love, whispering
To every single child—
Peace.

Every word, every touch
A blessed road homewards—
Peace.

Long sleep, deep space,
Fragrant after lovemaking—
Peace.

No more hope, it is
All in our hands—
Peace.

Herons and eagles
Beloved by the green river—
Peace.

Landfall and safety
After five hundred stormfronts—
Peace.

Two bluebirds asleep
In her sweater's pocket—
Peace.

In her mirror, arc
And comb of stars—
Peace.

At dawn, brushing
Long light across low mountains—
Peace.

Faith turns to astonishment
Turns to fact turns to trust—
Peace.

Sitting on a porch
With fox parents and pups—
Peace.

Deep in the desert hearing
Currents of a thousand clear rivers—
Peace.

Ink-dark wine, a fire,
Circulation of centuries—
Peace.

Beauty calling, bold,
Sure, unabashed, naked—
Peace.

Inside sentences, flashing
Of cheetahs in dreams—
Peace.

Every single word unfolded
With cosmic bemusement—
Peace.

★★★

Walking the street into
A swirling of worlds—
More real than real.

Cities are rivers
Are stars are words—
More real than real.

Love is earth is
Trust is journeywork—
More real than real.

We have been always
Where we are going—
More real than real.

We are now, where
We have been always—
More real than real.

Fate at the door, ardent,
Gift-giving, bright-souled—
More real than real.

No depth of playfulness
Like beckoning destiny—
More real than real.

Hunger is satiety
Is flying is homeground—
More real than real.

★★★

River thick with ice
Cracking in the sunlight—
On the move.

Lovers asleep
With wings wide open—
On the move.

Slow, patient, soaring,
Musky, devotional—
On the move.

Morning light the sidekick
Of long honest storytelling—
On the move.

Books, surety, talk
That polishes reality—
On the move.

Riding wild horses
Deep into good books—
On the move.

The whole ocean
Understands every raindrop—
On the move.

Coming together in friendship
With the jetstream—
On the move.

When talk is action is
Love is idea is life—
On the move.

By the hearth we burn,
To be made whole again—
On the move.

Just these many hours of
Luminosity and weightlessness—
On the move.

Planets can be
Moved by fingertips—
On the move.

Weaponry of the world made
Into kitchen tools—
On the move.

Homeland of allspice
In the middle of the night—
On the move.

Sacramental mischief
In the middle of the night—
On the move.

Lovemaking by candlelight
After life-making by sunlight—
On the move.

★★★

Animate canyons, mayflies,
Whirling of stars—
Come with me.

Rough devoted salty nights,
Days made of astonishment—
Come with me.

Making every choice
In league with dream—
Come with me.

Longer than time,
Faster than light—
Come with me.

Dropping by hell
To say goodbye—
Come with me.

In a book, hunger,
Clauses, hurricanes—
Come with me.

Here is my hand, you
Have had it always—
Come with me.

Let's make books from
Musk and starlight—
Come with me.

Here is my life, I
Have none other—
Come with me.

Rivers, grace, planets,
Candlelight, pampas—
Come with me.

All tropics in a touch,
Talk, dream, glance—
Come with me.

Because within this fidelity
Is the liberty of our dreams—
Come with me.

Let's leave honeycombs
Secretly, all over the world—
Come with me.

We must use the wings
We have made together—
Come with me.

Two rivers, this
Fine winged confluence—
Come with me.

Melting of souls to make
This fierce alloy—
    Come with me.

Lit bridges in big cities,
Stone bridges in villages—
    Come with me.

Rimrock and cougars,
Cabernet and long books—
    Come with me.

Lapis ocean, emerald
River, golden stone castles—
    Come with me.

Melting the steel of history
To build again—
    Come with me.

Naked talk, naked ideas,
Naked dreams, naked hours—
    Come with me.

Kissing whales, talking
With bobcats and young falcons—
Come with me.

Listening to starlight
And the foxes' footfall—
Come with me.

ACKNOWLEDGEMENTS

My thanks to Todd Swift, the head of Black Spring Press Group, for taking on an eccentric and rambling American writer; and to Amira Ghanim, for her professional support throughout this project. Special thanks to Catherine Myddleton-Evans for her careful, finely considered, insightful editorial comments on the manuscript.

I am in debt to the generous and knowledgeable Mary Bisbee-Beek for the introduction to Black Spring.

To my fellow writers in the United States, Europe, and the UK: thank you and bless you for your work. The fight for language of clarity and power is nothing less than the fight for civilization and survival.